TRUTH ABOUT LIES

DR. FREDERICK D. GORINI

Copyright © 2009 by Dr. Frederick D. Gorini

Truth About Lies

by Dr. Frederick D. Gorini

Printed in the United States of America

ISBN 978-1-60791-873-8

All rights reserved solely by the author. The author guarantees all contents are original and do not infringe upon the legal rights of any other person or work. No part of this book may be reproduced in any form without the permission of the author. The views expressed in this book are not necessarily those of the publisher.

Unless otherwise indicated, Bible quotations are taken from The New King James Version of the Bible. Copyright © 1982 by Thomas Nelson Publishers.

Other books by the Author:

BASKET-CASE BROTHERHOOD

THE INCARNATION OF TRUTH

TO THE UNKNOWN GOD
  The One whom you worship
  without knowing, Him I proclaim to you.

TRUTH BE TOLD
  A Sequel TO THE UNKNOWN GOD

www.xulonpress.com

This book is dedicated to Harold Vick
whom I met once forever.

TABLE OF CONTENTS

PROLOGUE:	GO, AND SIN NO MORE	ix
CHAPTER 1:	WHATEVER YOU DO	17
CHAPTER 2:	DISCOVER THE ROYAL RELATIONSHIP	27
CHAPTER 3:	CONQUER THE FIRST LIE	37
CHAPTER 4:	CONQUER THE SECOND LIE	43
CHAPTER 5:	CONQUER THE THIRD LIE	53
EPILOGUE:	TURN WATER TO WINE	61

PROLOGUE

GO AND SIN NO MORE

Therefore, if anyone is in Christ, he is a new creation; old things have passed away; behold, all things have become new.
2 Corinthians 5:17

When Jesus had raised Himself up and saw no one but the woman, He said to her, "Woman, where are those accusers of yours? Has no one condemned you?" She said, "No one Lord." And Jesus said to her, "Neither do I condemn you; go and sin no more."
John 8:10-11

Anyone that has received Jesus Christ as Lord and Savior has been made alive in Him with a new life. The Scripture calls it being "born again."[1] Because all men without Christ are considered by God to be dead in trespasses and sins,[2] Jesus taught that all people *must* be born again.[3]

This is a non-negotiable truth. Everyone ever born of blood, of the will of the flesh, and of the will of man,[4] has sinned and fallen short of the glory of God.[5] However, those that are now in Christ have been made free from the law of sin and death by the Spirit of life that is in Christ Jesus.⁶ According to the Word of God, there is now therefore no condemnation to those who walk according to the Spirit.⁷

This marvelous freedom from condemnation was foreshadowed in the Gospel of John, when the religious people of that day brought a woman caught in adultery to Jesus.⁸ They were testing Jesus to see if He would violate the law of Moses that required the death of such a sinner.⁹

The apostle John recorded that the crowd quickly dispersed as the wisdom of God came forth through the words and actions of Jesus. When the accusers saw what He wrote on the ground and heard Him speak; each of them—one by one—was convicted by their conscience. They realized that their own sin bound them to the same law of sin and subsequent death as the woman caught in adultery.¹⁰ To condemn her would seal the fate of their own condemnation.

Jesus did not condone the sin of the woman, but He did not condemn her either. Having eliminated the accusation against her, He applied the law of the Spirit of life to her situation saying, *"'Go and sin no more.'"*¹¹ This is the mandate for all New Testament believers that have been born of God.¹² Freedom from the law of sin and death is a marvelous part of the salvation provided for us in Christ. We do not have to sin!

Having liberated us from the law of sin and death, Jesus commanded those who follow Him to, *"'Go into all the world and preach the gospel* [good news] *to every creature.'"*¹³ He instructed all who follow Him: *"'Go and make disciples of all the nations.'"*¹⁴ Jesus also declared, *"'Freely you have received, freely give.'"*¹⁵

The plain and simple truth of the gospel, as preached by the Lord, makes it clear that those who abide in God's Word are His disciples. It is the knowledge of truth that makes us free.¹⁶ This New Testament freedom is more than just a philosophical concept. Those that are set free in Christ can actually live a life of freedom.

Jesus declared, *"'Therefore if the Son makes you free, you shall be free indeed.'"*[17] I like to think that "indeed" can be understood as "in deed!" This New Testament freedom from the law of sin and death is a reality that God's people can experience in this life. The apostle Paul exhorted the church to *"Stand fast therefore in the liberty by which Christ has made us free, and do not be entangled again with a yoke of bondage."*[18]

Now is a time for truth. If the church of the Lord Jesus Christ is really free, then why do so many still struggle with the sin issue in their lives? Why is it that the words of Jesus: "Go and sin no more" do not become a reality for so many?

Why do so few do what Jesus commanded? Why are there still so few laborers in the harvest field of the world?[19] Where are the multitudes of New Testament Christians that are for signs and wonders from the LORD of Hosts?[20] Why do we not rise up in the freedom of our new life in Christ, and do as He commanded? Why have so many, that have been made free by Christ, settled for a life of continuous struggle with the law of sin and death?

These things are so because we have believed the lies of the accuser of the brethren (Satan).[21] We fail to recognize that everything he ever communicates to us is a lie. The Word of God tells us that he is a murderer and a liar from the beginning and the truth is not in him. He is the father of lies.[22]

In the light of revealed present truth,[23] we are not to be ignorant of Satan's devices.[24] He has deceived us with lies that keep us bound and feeling condemned, contrary to the law of the Spirit of life that is in Christ Jesus. These lies can be considered to be the root of all of our bondage.

These lies keep us from doing the things that Jesus commanded in the freedom that He has provided. This is why there is so little manifestation of the power of the gospel unto salvation[25] in much of Christendom throughout the world. Revealing the truth about these lies will set us free to accomplish everything that the Lord has commanded us to do, both as a corporate expression of Christ, and as individual members in particular of His body.[26]

We can all experience this miraculous power in our daily lives. In failing to conquer the accuser's lies with the truth, we have allowed the Christian faith to be reduced to a gospel of life after death. We have allowed "now" to be substituted by "later." Of course, we thank God that once our earth lives are completed, we go to be in the presence of the Lord forever.[27]

However, the Christian faith is not only good news about life after death; it also includes life after birth! Those who have been born again, born of God,[28] born from above—have received the power of the Holy Spirit[29] to be more than conquerors[30] in *this* life and also in that which is to come.[31]

The key to the release of miraculous power in this life was foreshadowed in the Gospel of John just as freedom from sin was in the account of the adulterous woman. At the wedding at Cana of Galilee, where Jesus did the impossible and turned water into wine,[32] a powerful revelation of miracle producing truth is found. Mary, the mother of Jesus, instructed the servants saying, *"'Whatever He says to you, do it.'"*[33]

This is the key to the release of miraculous power. Whatever *He* says to you, do it! The blessing, the miracle power, is released through our obedience to His Word. A doer of the Word is blessed not by what he knows, but in what he does.[34] The apostle James instructed us to be doers of the word and not hearers only. By just hearing and not doing what we have heard we deceive ourselves.[35] Faith without works is dead.[36] Freedom "indeed" must become freedom "in deed!"

Christianity without active faith has no Christ life in it. It becomes a dead religion producing no proof that Jesus Christ is alive.[37] Without evidence, without a faithful and true witness of the new life in Christ,[38] free from the law of sin and death in this life, many souls remain condemned and suffer in their struggle with trespasses and sins.

Why then, do we not just awake from our religious sleep and arise from the dead so that Christ will give us light?[39] Why do we continue struggling with the law of sin and death? Why do we not do as Jesus told the woman: *"Go and sin no more"*?

It is because we have believed the lies of the devil. He tells us that we cannot do it. In our daily lives he confronts us just as he did when he tempted Jesus in the wilderness. Satan mockingly taunts us with thoughts that question our freedom, our ability, and our identity in Christ.

Satan taunted Jesus as if to say, "If you are the Son of God—prove it by doing what seems impossible."[40] Is it possible for a man to turn stones into bread? Can a man throw himself down from the pinnacle of a high building without incurring death or serious injury? Such were the taunts of Satan hurled at Jesus during the temptation in the wilderness.

That was then, this is now. Today Satan taunts *us* using the pressure and stress of life in this modern world system. He attempts to make us believe that we really can't live the Christian life here and now. He is a liar. In Christ, and through His strength, we can do all things.[41] We must take every thought captive to the obedience of Christ.[42]

As you read through these pages you will discover the truth about Satan's lies. The accuser of the brethren uses three great lies in his attempt to undermine the truth of the gospel that has been revealed to us through our Lord Jesus Christ. Simply put these three lies are:

- You just cannot do it (live the Christ life).
- It's too hard; just quit.
- It's just not worth it.

We have all heard these lies. They are sequential. Once you conquer the first lie that deceives you into thinking you are not free to do what God has commanded, you can expect the enemy to attack you with another lie. Haven't you ever heard the tempter whisper "It's too hard; just quit"? That is a satanic thought and an absolute lie against the truth.

Once you've conquered this second lie and refuse to quit, think it not strange if you are challenged to quench another fiery dart of the devil with your shield of faith.[43] How many times have you been tempted by the thought, "It's just not worth it"? This too, is a lie inspired by the devil.

Fear not, dear brothers and sisters; as you continue reading you will come to the knowledge of the truth and be able to conquer all three of these lies, and all the others that spring from the root system of deception created by them.

Start collecting your thoughts. What specific assignments has the Lord prescribed for you in this life? Identify them. List them. It's time you revisited all of them. Rehearse them in your heart and mind and get ready to fulfill them all.

Before we deal specifically with these three lies of the devil I am going to lay a very important foundation for you, on which to build a library of truth. This will enable us all to stand against the wiles of the devil, and to withstand in the evil day, and having done all, to remain standing.[44] It is time to do what the Word of God says,

> *Watch, stand fast in the faith, be brave, be strong.*[45] *Submit to God. Resist the devil and he will flee from you.*[46] *Resist him steadfast in the faith.*[47] *Stand fast therefore in the liberty by which Christ has made us*

free, and do not be entangled again with a yoke of bondage.[48]

In other words, *"Go and sin no more."*[49] Is it that simple? Yes it is. Being in Christ, there is therefore now no condemnation. Walk according to the light of His Word, according to His gracious Holy Spirit and be free from the law of sin and death. Just do it!

If you know these things,
blessed are you if you do them.
John 13:17

PROLOGUE: GO AND SIN NO MORE

Main Points:

- When a person is "born again" they receive a new life in Christ.
- Those in Christ are made free from the law of sin and death.
- There is now, no condemnation for those in Christ.
- All believers are free to go into all the world and preach the gospel.
- Many Christians do not do what Jesus commanded and still struggle with the sin issue in their lives.
- The lies of the devil are what keep us from doing the will of God.
- The truth of God's Word can conquer the devil's lies.
- The devil uses three basic lies to stop God's people from doing His will:
  —You just cannot do it.
  —It's too hard; just quit.
  —It's just not worth it.
- By doing God's will you can be free to fulfill His purpose for your life.
- If you know these things and do them, you will be blessed.

CHAPTER 1

WHATEVER YOU DO

Blessed is the man . . . . his delight is in the law of the LORD, *And in His law he meditates day and night . . . . And whatever he does shall prosper.*
Psalm 1:1-3 excerpts

A doer of the work, this one will be blessed in what he does.
James 1:25b

The blessing of God is released through the doing of His will. Jesus Himself declared, *"'Behold, I have come— In the volume of the book it is written of Me—To do Your will, O God.'"*[1] Doing the will of God is the key to prosperity in a believer's life. The LORD takes pleasure in the prosperity of His servant.[2] The fulfillment of the LORD's will significantly magnifies Him and facilitates making Him known to the lost.[3]

Jesus declared that He did nothing of Himself, but always spoke and did the things that pleased the Father.[4] On more than one occasion the Father opened the heavens declaring, *"'This is My beloved Son in whom I am well pleased.'"*[5]

The Father's pleasure is the source of miracle power and a guarantee of blessing for the one who does the will of God. Jesus knew that without the Father's blessing He could do nothing.[6] Fulfilling the will of the Father enabled Jesus to do the great works that provide salvation and blessing for whosoever will believe.[7]

It is the same for us concerning the valid witness of the glory of the life of God *in* us. Jesus made it clear that only by abiding in Him (the Word of God) can we bear fruit that will glorify the Father.[8] He said,

"I am the vine, you are the branches. He who abides in Me, and I in him, bears much fruit; for without Me you can do nothing."[9]

Abiding in Christ is the source of our ability to do even greater works than He did. Jesus promised that we would receive such ability.[10] This is an astounding truth of New Testament life in the kingdom of God. It is the Father's good pleasure to give us (as the corporate, many membered body of Christ) the kingdom—in which the will of God is done on earth as it is in heaven.[11]

So what is it that you are doing with *your* life? Don't let the devil stop you! I assure you that you can do the will of God and completely fulfill the purpose for which you have been given the gift of life. Each one of us in the body of Christ is a member in particular,[12] a unique expression of God Himself and of His Son, the Lord Jesus Christ.[13] You can be sure that He has chosen you and appointed you to make Him known.[14]

Psalm 1 declares that as you meditate and delight yourself in the Word of God, *whatever* you do will prosper.[15] What a promise! As a man, husband, father—a woman, wife, mother—a son or daughter—you will be blessed as you do the will of God.[16] You will be blessed in whatever you do![17]

Some are called to the business world, some to the ministry. Some are called to be teachers, some are students in training. Some are called to be doctors or nurses, some lawyers. Some are called to be employers, some serve as employees. All of the callings in life have corresponding activities that are necessary in order to fulfill the purpose for which they were created.

What are *you* called to be—or called to do? You can do it! Christianity is not about what you cannot do. It is all about what you can do, in Christ. It is His will and power that enable you to do all things that He has planned for you.[18] In Him, whatever it is that you do, will prosper. This is gospel truth.

There's a secret revealed in the Scriptures that will change your life if you will just get up and do it—whatever 'it' is. Paul wrote to the church in Colosse and said,

And whatever you do in word or deed, do all in the name of the Lord Jesus, giving thanks to God the Father through Him.[19]

To act in the name of Jesus is to exercise the delegated authority given to each of us as the children of God.[20] It is like having the power of attorney of the name of Jesus. His name is above all names and the proper use of it will bring everything into divine order.[21] There is no other name under heaven by which men can be saved.[22] The salvation of souls is the ultimate fruit of whatever any of us do.[23]

Jesus is called, *"The author and finisher of our faith."*[24] This declaration provides evidence that whatever we do in His name is the authorized version of our lives and anything we do apart from Him is unauthorized. Whatever we do in His name is the work of our faith—which comes by hearing His Word.[25] Because it is the authorized version, it is full of

His authority and power. Think about it. Meditate on this and whatever you do in His name will prosper!

As wonderful as this revelation of truth is, there is more—much more that follows those who act in the name of Jesus. When you live the authorized version of your life, it is not only whatever you do that will prosper, but following the same scriptural principles, *wherever* you go to do whatever you do—you will prosper! The LORD promised Joshua that if he would meditate on the Word of God both day and night—just as revealed to David when he wrote Psalm 1—he would make his way prosperous and have good success wherever he went.[26]

What promises! There is still more—much more! In truth, this double blessing of whatever you do—wherever you go, is actually a threefold cord that once braided is not easily broken.[27] These promises are for *whoever* will believe. It is written,

> *"For God so loved the world that He gave His only begotten Son, that whoever believes in Him should not perish but have everlasting life."*[28]

Wow! The promises of God include *whatever, wherever,* for *whoever*—what a life! It is the living of this authorized life that enables us to give thanks to God the Father through Jesus the Son.[29] When we give thanks we enter the gates of the dwelling place of God and come before the presence of the LORD.[30] In His presence there is fullness of joy.[31] Yes, whatever you do in the name of the Lord Jesus, gives thanks to God the Father through Him.[32] It is good to give thanks to the LORD.[33] Giving thanks to God is no small thing. In the New Testament, the apostle Paul said it like this,

> *Now thanks be to God who always leads us in triumph in Christ, and through us diffuses the fragrance of His knowledge in every place.*[34]

What a revelation. Let's examine it and compare it to the biblical concepts we are establishing.

We can meditate on the words "triumph in Christ" and compare them to the "whatever you do will prosper" promise of God. We can meditate on the words "every place" and compare them to the "wherever you go" promise of God. We can also meditate on the multiple use of the word "us" and compare it to the "whoever will believe" promise of God. In other words, we could say that in Christ we triumph in whatever we do, sharing His presence wherever we go, with everyone we meet! This is an awesome God thought. This is biblical truth! This is part of the normal New Testament Christian life.

Finally, we can meditate on the word "always" and compare it to the promise of God that says, *"When a man's ways please the* LORD, *He makes even his enemies to be at peace with him."*[35] The word "always" is a powerful time and space, here, now and forever concept. It includes every "when."

When is always? Or better said than asked—"When is always!" "Always" is *whenever* you do the will of God. Your faith actions are pleasing to the LORD, just as the Scripture says, *"Without faith it is impossible to please Him."*[36]

You can actually know that the Lord is pleased with you. The Scripture says, *"By this I know that You* [God] *are well pleased with me, Because my enemy does not triumph over me."*[37] Glory to God! Yes, you can live this kind of victorious life and diffuse the fragrance of His knowledge in every place. As you do all in the name of Jesus, whatever you do will prosper. Wherever you go, you can share His life with whoever you meet. Whenever you do this you will walk in victory.

There's another secret that will change your life if you will just get up and do it—whatever 'it' is. In his epistle to the church at Colosse, Paul also said, *"And whatever you do, do it heartily, as to the Lord and not to men."*[38] This is an essential part of victorious truth. It is a deep heart issue.

Someone has called this, "living before an audience of one."[39] Everything we do should be done for Him. Our motive should always be that His will is done.[40] It really is of no consequence what anyone else thinks. We can be totally free from the fear of man and should never be motivated by what others think of us, except as it relates to our living witness of Christ.

For the promises of God to become a reality to us, whatever we do, we must do it with our whole heart. To be halfhearted is to be lukewarm and displeasing to the Lord.[41] God has purposed that our lives are to bring Him glory.[42] He is worthy of *all* of our praise.[43] The psalmist said, *"I will praise You, O LORD, with my whole heart; I will tell of all Your marvelous works."*[44]

Whatever we do in word and deed, either magnifies or diminishes the LORD in the eyes of those who observe our lives. To tell of the works of the LORD in a halfhearted way, diminishes Him in the eyes of those we testify to. When we praise the LORD and all of His great works with our whole heart, it causes others to study the Word of God and seek out the blessing that is released as they become doers of it.[45]

The great commandment of God that sums up all the law and the prophets has to do with the whole heart.[46] We are commanded to love the LORD God with all of our hearts, all of our souls, and all of our minds.[47] Anything less than offering love to God with our whole heart is self destructive and a poor witness to our neighbors, whom we are to love also.[48]

Many do not realize that this first and great commandment is found in the Old Testament as well as in the New. It is not found in the Ten Commandments given to Moses on Mount Sinai, but it is found in God's instruction to His people with regard to assuring the generational blessing of being in covenant with Him.

The LORD commanded His people, including their children and grandchildren, to be careful to hear and obey the mighty declaration of the great commandment. He said,

"Hear, O Israel: The LORD our God, the LORD is one! You shall love the LORD your God with all your heart, with all your soul, and with all your might."[49]

These are the words that God instructed His people to teach diligently to their children. These are the words to be taught when sitting at home, when doing business in the community, when going to sleep and rising up.[50] These are the words to be kept before our eyes and fulfilled with the work of our hands.[51] Whatever we do, we are to do it with the whole heart as to the Lord, and not to men.

There is no substitute for obeying God with the whole heart. To do anything in God's kingdom with less than the whole heart can be considered evil. The prophet Malachi addressed the way the Old Testament people of God offended Him by reducing the measure of their service to Him.

The LORD described their behavior as dishonorable and without proper reverence for Him, actually a despicable use of His name.[52] When the priests asked for an explanation the LORD responded using such words as, *"You offer defiled food on My altar . . . . you offer the blind, the lame and the sick to Me."*[53] In New Testament language we could say that they were lukewarm or halfhearted in what they were doing.

The LORD then challenged them to offer such sacrifices to their governor and see if he would be pleased with them.[54] We could liken such a statement to trying to pay the IRS only half of what is due them. If that is what you do, you can be sure that your half-heartedness (sin) will be found out.[55] There is no substitute for doing whatever we do, with our whole heart as to the Lord and not to men.

The wisdom of the Proverbs commands us saying, *"Keep your heart with all diligence, for out of it spring the issues of life."*[56] You can be sure that as you do all in the name of Jesus, with your whole heart, that you will be blessed in whatever you do.[57] In so doing, you will be honoring the Lord Jesus Christ and God the Father. May the Holy Spirit of God lead you into fulfilling God's Word for your life that you may truly be known as a child of God.[58]

The ultimate revelation that convinces the world that we are indeed (in deed) disciples of Jesus and children of God is our love for one another.[59] This love is part of, and a continuation of, the great commandment to love the LORD with our whole heart. It is the second great commandment of the New Testament.[60]

Whatever we do in word or in deed, whether loving God or loving people, we are to do it with the whole heart. In so doing we fulfill what the Scriptures call the *"royal law."*[61] This is what we are called to do.

Remember, He chose you, you did not choose Him.[62] According to God's Word, we are a chosen generation, a *royal* priesthood, a holy nation, His own special people.[63] As God's people we are His royal family. Let's act like it. Go and sin no more and whatever you do shall prosper.

> *But he who looks into the perfect law of liberty and continues in it, and is not a forgetful hearer but a doer of the work, this one will be blessed in what he does. If you really fulfill the royal law according to the Scripture, "You shall love your neighbor as yourself," you do well.*
> James 1:25, 2:8

CHAPTER 1: WHATEVER YOU DO

Main Points:

- A doer of God's will is blessed in what he does.
- As one meditates on God's Word, whatever he does will prosper.
- Christianity is about what you can do—not what you cannot do.
- All that we do should be done in the name of Jesus.
- As one meditates on God's Word, wherever he goes he will prosper.
- These promises are for whoever will believe.
- When a man's ways please the LORD, He makes even his enemies to be at peace with him.
- Whatever you do, do it heartily as to the Lord and not to men.
- Keep your heart with all diligence.
- Doers of God's Word are a part of His chosen, royal family.
- Loving one's neighbor fulfills the royal law.

CHAPTER 2

DISCOVER THE ROYAL RELATIONSHIP

"Has not the Scripture said that the Christ comes from the seed of David and from the town of Bethlehem, where David was?"
John 7:42

And everyone who was in distress, everyone who was in debt, and everyone who was discontented gathered to him. So he [David] became captain over them. And there were about four hundred men with him.
1 Samuel 22:2

It is time to discover the royal relationship we have with God through Christ our King. In this chapter I am going to lead you into the final phase of preparation before conquering the lies of Satan with the truth of God's Word. Truth is a person. Truth is the person of Jesus.[1] Jesus is the only begotten of the Father, full of grace and truth.[2] He is God's ordained King of kings and Lord of lords.[3] Jesus is the royal Son of God.[4]

Although Jesus Christ our Lord is the only begotten of the Father, He is not God's only offspring. The Scripture declares that Jesus is the firstborn of many brethren.[5] He is bringing many children of God to glory.[6] The distinction between "only" and "firstborn" is extremely important.

Jesus prayed that the Father would sanctify us by the Word of truth (Jesus Himself).[7] The Scripture declares that He who sanctifies and those who are being sanctified are all of One, and therefore He is not ashamed to call us brethren.[8] This is an amazing revelation! In and through Christ we are part of God's royal family. Jesus is not ashamed of us!

Jesus declared to the Father, *"Here am I and the children whom God has given Me."*[9] This is a quote from the Old Testament prophet Isaiah who declared that we, God's children, are for signs and wonders in the earth.[10] We should not be running after signs and wonders, they should be following us![11]

God has always used living men, women, and children to display signs and wonders of the glory of His own image and likeness. I call it the personification of His royal nature. Jesus Christ is of course, the first and last word of the revelation of God's own express image.[12] We are to fix our eyes on Him, the author and finisher of our faith.[13]

To help us see the revelation of Jesus Christ more clearly, I would like to refer to three Old Testament men that stand out above all the heroes of the faith in the days before the incarnation of the Word. There are so many great personifications of God in the Old Testament that prophetically exemplify the Christ life of the New Testament. We could refer to Noah, Joseph, Moses, or Elijah. Any one of these could accurately personify God's image and likeness. We could choose Deborah, Ruth, or Esther and clearly see the royal nature of God personified. However, there are three Old Testament men that stand above them all.

First there is Adam, then Abraham, and last but certainly not least there is David the king. I have chosen these three above all others for precise scriptural reasons.

Jesus the Christ is called the Son of Man (Adam).[14] He is also called the Seed of Abraham,[15] as well as both the son of David[16] and the seed of David.[17] These titles all reveal very significant relationships in the genealogy of our Lord Jesus Christ.

The relationship between Jesus Christ and these three men is a prototype of our relationship to them, and through the testimony of their lives, to Him. By our natural birth we are all related to Adam *racially*. All of us who have been born again in the Christian faith are related to Abraham *redemptively*. Subsequently, now that we are experiencing new life in the kingdom of God on earth, we are all related to David *royally*.

As I explain these relationships in greater detail, keep in mind what has already been established as the pattern for all we do in this life. Whatever we do, we are to do it heartily as to the Lord and not to men.[18]

Jesus Christ is our royal Lord.[19] I am going to magnify His royalty and Lordship through the use of *hindsight* relating to specific Old Testament historical accounts of God's people. This will give us *insight* into Christ's power in our present lives and *foresight* into the future of His kingdom.

The Old Testament is filled with stories that are real—they are not fairy tales. They were recorded as examples for us, on whom the end of the ages have come.[20] These stories are factual accounts of how God's power and anointing enabled men, women, and children of faith to rise above every circumstance and situation. They lived their lives as unto the LORD and because of His greatness, they became great.

The first is Adam. He stands above all others because in the beginning he was the first and only man.[21] Everyone ever born has been born of the race of Adam. Even Jesus, our Lord, was born of a woman and entered this world the same way that all others have with the exception of the first man and woman.[22] As I have already noted, Jesus is called the Son of Man (Adam).[23]

There are really only two races of man on planet earth. Race is not based on color. It never has been. Originally there was only one Adamic race and every human being was born into that race. This is why Adam stands above all others in the Old Testament.

When Adam sinned the entire Adamic race came under the influence and consequence of sin.[24] Man became mortal and subject to death.[25] Instead of bringing forth offspring in the image of God in which he was created, a careful reading of the Scripture reveals that all of Adam's offspring were brought forth in his own fallen image.[26]

This is the reason why human beings need a new creation race. It has nothing to do with color. To call a man black, white, red, or yellow simply describes his earth suit — the house of his spirit and soul. Just like houses, cars, and other things come in different colors, so also does man.

It was because of the sin nature that Adam passed to all his generations that God sent another man. He sent the Eternal Word as the Incarnate Word into the race of fallen man.[27] This man was born of a virgin.[28] His father was not Adam; His father was and is God.[29] Yet He entered this world through the womb of a woman so that He could be the Son of Man. Jesus Christ is called the second Man and the last Adam.[30]

Through His death, burial, and resurrection, Jesus Christ became the firstborn from the dead,[31] paying in full for the consequence of Adamic sin. He created a brand new race — the generation of Jesus Christ![32]

There are only two races of men. The Scripture is emphatic about the origin of all men. In the apostle Paul's great discourse to the ancient Greek philosophers he cried out, *"'He* [God] *has made from one blood every nation of men to dwell on all the face of the earth . . .'"*[33]

Whether men are black, white, red, or yellow, they are all of the same blood. Race is based on blood and every human being ever born is related to Adam by blood. Thank God that now there is a new man—the second Man, the last Adam that has redeemed us to God by His own sinless blood![34] Those who have been forgiven of their sins through the power of Christ's blood have been redeemed and are now a new creation, a part of the generation of Jesus Christ.[35]

This redemption I am referring to brings us to the next great man of the Old Testament—Abraham. Everyone that is a part of this new generation in Christ is related to Abraham redemptively. Abraham is called the father of the faith.[36] Jesus Christ is called the Seed of Abraham.[37]

Long ago God chose Abraham out of Ur of the Chaldees.[38] Abraham was of the sinful race of Adam, as were all men at that time. The LORD promised to reward Abraham's obedience to His Word if he would walk before Him and be blameless.[39]

Abraham believed God and it was accounted to him for righteousness.[40] The blessing of Abraham's faith was to affect the entire Adamic race. God promised that in Abraham's seed *all* the families and nations of the earth would be blessed.[41]

God established a sacrificial blood covenant with Abraham and with his Seed.[42] That Seed was Jesus Christ[43] and through the shedding of His innocent blood, the redemption of the race of Adam was secured.[44] This redemption is for whoever will believe.[45]

Yes, all men by natural birth are related to Adam *racially*. All men of the new creation, by faith in God and the power of Christ's blood, are related to Abraham *redemptively*. Finally, as members of the generation of Jesus Christ all men are related to David *royally*! This is a very important concept.

David was God's Old Testament chosen king—a man after God's own heart.[46] David was a prototype of the Lord Jesus Christ. Jesus is called the Son of David[47] and the seed of David.[48] This is the beginning of the revelation of the *royal* family.

We could paraphrase Paul's instruction to the church at Colosse saying, "And whatever you do, do it *royally* with your whole heart as to the King and not to men."[49] In Christ we are all royalty. The power of His royal blood has redeemed us to God, has also made us to be kings and priests to our God, and has granted unto us power and authority to live royally, and reign with Him on the earth![50]

It is not a trite cliché to say that we are "king's kids." This is the truth of God's Word. Without an understanding of such truth we will struggle to conquer the lies that the devil attacks us with. The new generation in Christ really is a royal race.

According to the apostle Peter we are a holy nation, a royal priesthood, God's own special people.[51] This is why King David stands above other Old Testament characters that personify the Christ. It is King David that represents the royalty of the Lord Jesus Christ.

There is something very significant about true royalty. Do not think of earthly kings or monarchs and their families. Without Christ they are simply the children of Adam. As you read think of our Lord Jesus Christ and the royal family of God.

Something happens to ordinary people when they are around true royalty. There is something special that happens when ordinary people do whatever they do in the King's name, with their whole heart, because of love for Him and not for recognition by men.

The royal nature of the King brings out the *best* from the worst, the *strongest* from the weakest, and the *most* from the least. Mark these words well; it is in the revelation brought by these words that we will find our victory over satanic lies.

As members of the Adamic race weren't we all among the worst, the weakest, and the least? In the light of divine royalty, these human conditions are shared by all fallen men whether they acknowledge it to be so or not. These characteristics should not be viewed as permanent liabilities, but simply temporary handicaps prior to becoming a member of the new redeemed and royal race.

The apostle Paul said that God calls men to Himself when they are not wise, not mighty, and not noble.[52] In fact, Paul said that God has chosen the foolish things, the weak things, the base things, the despised things, and things that are nothing so that no flesh would glory in His (royal) presence.[53]

This is the royal way. This magnificent ability of Jesus Christ to transform the lowly lives of fallen men was so clearly portrayed and personified in the life of King David. It is written,

And everyone who was in distress, everyone who was in debt, and everyone who was discontented gathered to him. And he became captain over them.[54]

In what are called David's wilderness years as he fled from King Saul, David attracted the lowest, neediest people around. Saul was still the King of Israel even though the prophet Samuel had already anointed David to replace him.[55] David was the true king, the true royalty.

The anointing of royalty on David's life was so strong that he was able to gather the outcasts of this world and transform them to greatness by his own royal character. Their association with David brought out the best from the worst, the strongest from the weakest, and the most from the least. The history of this royal relationship is a prophetic revelation of the New Testament Church.

This is the key to conquering the lies of the devil in your own life. Your association with the royalty of Jesus Christ will make you great. Royalty can make somebody out of anybody. You qualify! Discovering the royal relationship of Christ and His church will make you more than a conqueror in this life.[56] Armed with the truth, let's read on and conquer the devil's lies. Let's just do it!

I will build my church, and the gates of Hades shall not prevail against it.
Matthew 16:18

CHAPTER 2: DISCOVER THE ROYAL RELATIONSHIP

Main Points:

- Truth is the person of Jesus Christ.
- Through Christ we are a part of God's royal family.
- The royal nature is personified in the lives of the saints.
- We are all related to Adam racially.
- People of the faith are related to Abraham redemptively, and to David royally.
- There are only two races of men—the Adamic race and the generation of Jesus Christ.
- All human beings can be redeemed by the blood of Jesus.
- The generation of Jesus Christ is a royal generation.
- The royal nature brings out the best from the worst, the strongest from the weakest, and the most from the least.
- Association with the royalty of Jesus Christ will make you great.
- Association with royalty can make somebody out of anybody.
- You qualify!

CHAPTER 3
CONQUER THE FIRST LIE

But He said, "The things which are impossible with men are possible with God."
Luke 18:27

These are the names of the mighty men whom David had: Josheb-Basshebeth the Tachmonite, chief among the captains. He was called Adino the Eznite, because he had killed eight hundred men at one time.
2 Samuel 23:8

Eight hundred against one? Impossible! The odds are against you. You just cannot do it. What a lie—a satanic lie. As you read apply this principle of truth to your own relationship with Christ the King.

This lie is a greater lie than it seems to be when you consider the historical time in which Adino the Eznite, the chief captain of David's mighty men lived. Back then there were no such weapons as used by today's Terminator or Rambo. Men fought with not much more than sticks and stones. Spears, swords, axes, and knives were the best weapons of the day. Can you picture it?

Yet, Adino the Eznite did it. He conquered overwhelming odds by killing eight hundred men at one time. The Bible does not give us the details. They are not that important. What is important is that against all odds Adino was able to do what could be considered impossible.

Adino the Eznite was not even an Israelite. He was not of the royal blood and family of David. He was a Tachmonite. Where was Tachmon? Nobody knows. He was a nobody, from nowhere.

Adino was probably among the most rag-tag outlaws of his day. He was among those distressed, in debt, and discontented foreigners who were gathered unto David in the wilderness, and may have been the worst of them.[1] Yet, he became the chief captain of David's mighty men through an act of greatness.

What was it that made this man the best among the worst? It was his association with the royal heart of King David. What others could not or would not do—he did. It is obvious from the circumstances (eight hundred against one), that he must have acted with his whole heart on behalf of his king.

The devil lies to us making us think that it is impossible to live the life that King Jesus has promised us. It is against all odds. Not so. Not when you have a relationship with royalty.

This story in the Bible is not a fairy tale, nor is Adino a comic book hero from yesterday. In fact, this story is not really about him at all. Read in context, it is about King David and the men who became mighty through relationship with him. Spiritually understood it is really an example for us of our relationship with Jesus Christ.[2]

This story is a pre-scription (written before) for us, in order to teach us the benefits of being rightly related to the King.[3] It brings us comfort and hope. This story is written to tell the truth about the lie that you cannot do what God wants you to do.

Have you ever heard about "the facts of life"? I am going to tell you the truth about the facts of life. This truth will conquer the devil's lie that makes you believe you cannot overcome the odds stacked against you in this life.

It is not possible that your life is a mistake. No matter whom your parents were, or the circumstances of your conception—you can believe that your life came from God. He gave it to you through your parents, but it came from Him. God is the only source of life. He Himself is life.[4] God was there at the moment of your conception. Even if your parents were doing something outside of what God might consider covenant behavior, He was there.

Sexual encounters take place all over the world, all the time. Sexual activity between a man and a woman does not always lead to conception. Conception is a miracle of God. Only He can give life. Let me tell you the truth about the odds against your own conception, and the seemingly impossible task it took for you to overcome the odds.

You were conceived at the finish line of a race. The race began at a special moment when the waters of potential life were released in a climactic explosion. These waters were carrying something called seed, or more accurately, "sperma."

The race was only a few inches long.[5] The seeds were all microscopic, and all of them were racing to obtain the prize—the fertilization of one egg. Just one![6] Once one sperm reached the finish line—the egg—God had designed the egg to put up a wall of impenetrable protection so there could only be one winner.[7] All the others in the race would die. Their existence would be over forever.

What were the odds against you? Modern science has verified what God knew all along. At the moment those waters of life were shot forth and the race began, there were as many as five hundred million seeds released![8] Only one made it. You!

Against all odds—because the LORD God authored it, you were conceived! Five hundred million to one—and you won! There is no way anyone can call that a mistake. There is no way to call you a loser. There is no way to declare that you "just cannot do it." You already did it!

Any one of those millions of other seeds could have won, but didn't. You did! Had any of the others won you would not be you. A brother or sister might have been conceived, but certainly not you. Against all odds *you* made it. You were conceived a winner.

These are not just facts of life. This is the truth that conquers the lie of Satan that says to you, "There's no way. You just can't do it. It's impossible. The odds are against you."

The truth is God knew you at the moment of conception. The Word of the LORD came to Jeremiah the prophet and revealed a secret about God's involvement with his conception. God said, *"'Before I formed you in the womb* [in seed form] *I knew you.'"*[9]

God is no respecter of persons,[10] and He shows no partiality. If He knew Jeremiah, I believe He also knew me—and you, before we were formed in the womb. The New Testament confirms that the LORD shows no favoritism of one person over another in at least four passages.[11]

In fact, the New Testament indicates that if *we* show partiality we commit sin, and are convicted as transgressors of His law.[12] Does God violate His own Word? Certainly not—He does not favor one person over another. With the possible exception of Esau (some might also include Judas or Pharaoh) it is evident that God loves all people the same. As we have already noted, the Word of God declares that when a person loves a neighbor with the same measure as they love themselves, they fulfill *"the royal law."*[13]

God is not partial, but He does respond favorably to faith. Come to Him in faith. Don't be stopped by the odds that are against you in this life. Approach Him believing that He is, and that He is a rewarder of those who diligently seek Him.[14]

Not only did God know you before conception, He knew you intimately while you were being formed in your mother's womb.[15] It was there and then that He scripted and ordained your victory in this life.[16] That is the truth. The psalmist wrote,

> *I will praise You, for I am fearfully and wonderfully made; Marvelous are Your works, And that my soul knows very well. My frame was not hidden from You, When I was made in secret, And skillfully wrought in the lowest parts of the earth. Your eyes saw my substance, being yet unformed. And in Your book they all were written, The days fashioned for me, When as yet there were none of them.*[17]

Just do it. Believe the Word of God. He even knew that you would be reading this book today. You are a winner! You can do all things through Christ who strengthens you.[18] All of God's thoughts toward you are precious. The sum of them is great.[19] This is not a dream, nor is it a fantasy. Shake yourself and wake up to the truth. You will find that God is still with you and for you, as He always has been.[20]

The greatness of King Jesus and His royal nature will bring out the best in you. He brings out the best from the worst. Knowing Him and the truth about your royal heritage in Christ conquers Satan's lie. You can do it. You are doing it already. Yes, you are!

> *The people who know their God shall be strong, and carry out great exploits.*
> Daniel 11:32b

CHAPTER 3: CONQUER THE FIRST LIE

Main Points:

- With God all things are possible.
- It is a lie of the devil that says you cannot live the victorious Christian life as God has ordained.
- God can bring forth the best from the worst.
- The truth about the facts of life is that you were conceived as a winner.
- At conception you conquered overwhelming odds.
- God shows no partiality to men.
- God was intimately involved in your conception and birth, and remains with you in this life.
- You can do all things through Christ who strengthens you.

CHAPTER 4

CONQUER THE SECOND LIE

For you have need of endurance, so that after you have done the will of God, you may receive the promise.
Hebrews 10:36

And after him was Eleazar the son of Dodo, the Ahohite, one of the three mighty men with David when they defied the Philistines who were gathered there for battle, and the men of Israel had retreated.
2 Samuel 23:9

So—you went ahead and did it. Against all odds you stepped up and stepped out and did the right thing—the God thing. You acted in faith with your whole heart as to the Lord, defying the lie of the enemy. The blessings of God began to flow.

You experienced a great sense of satisfaction and thanksgiving as you obeyed the Lord and conquered the things that war against the soul.[1] Others even began to follow your example as they observed your good works and glorified God with you.[2]

This is what the apostle Peter, the man who walked on water,[3] taught in his epistles, written to those who have obtained like precious faith by the righteousness of our Lord Jesus Christ.[4] He even taught that the conduct of a righteous person who obeyed the Lord, would win over others to the same kind of faith.[5] Peter said that words wouldn't even be necessary to convince others to follow such a life of victory and freedom.[6] The good example would be sufficient to encourage others to do what they once thought to be impossible and against all odds.

Our own life experience bears this truth out. In gymnastics there was a time when no one thought multiple somersaults with one leap was possible. After someone got up and did it, it no longer seemed to be as impossible as it once was. Nowadays, every world class gymnast can do it. It is the same with running a mile in less than four minutes. Once one man broke the barrier, many others followed. Our world is filled with good examples of overcoming impossible odds. Once someone does it, others follow.

The fact that something once deemed impossible has now been done, doesn't mean that it's easy. Gymnasts and runners must maintain their training and disciplined lifestyle in order to continue mastering the challenges they have conquered. It is the same in the spiritual world.

Just because you did it—*whatever* it is that you did—to the Lord with your whole heart, doesn't mean the challenge is over. Endurance is necessary for the fullness of the promised blessing to become a reality in your life.[7]

Have you noticed that many people start to do something good, something great, and something wonderful for God with their whole hearts, but few ever finish? One could think of natural things such as walking away from smoking, drinking, cursing, anger, depression, and a myriad of other detrimental life activities as examples. Many well meaning people defy the odds and begin to be free, but so many do not maintain the blessing of freedom.

It is even more challenging with deeper spiritual things. It is not so hard to love someone who is unloving, or to be patient with them for a little while. Most of us can be kind to someone for a season; but what happens as time passes and we don't see the results that we were promised in God's Word? So often, time wears us down.

How long does the Lord expect us to be sexually pure in a world full of sexual immorality? The onslaught is incredible. How long does the Lord expect us to uphold the standard of the sanctity of life in the face of millions of abortions? Are we making a difference at all? Why should we continue to be honest about paying our taxes when it is obvious that our own governmental leaders are so corrupt? Thoughts like these come to us all.

Dear one, I assure you that *after* you have done the will of God and conquered lie number one, there is another lie that the enemy hurls at you; "Just quit!" You know you've heard it time and time again. "Just quit!"

Such words open the door to a multitude of false communications. You begin to think things like, "It's too hard." Then you begin to look around at how others are handling the lie. Although you started by doing whatever you did as to the Lord and not to men, after a while what others are doing begins to draw your attention and divide your heart.

What are so many others doing? Look around, so many of them are throwing in the towel. They tell you, "Life is much easier now that I've quit. The Lord understands. He doesn't really expect us to be perfect." Haven't you heard something like this—if not from others, certainly in your own thought life? "Just quit!"

What a lie! Is there a scriptural example that can help us find our way into truth and conquer this lie? Yes, there is. King David's mighty man Eleazar the son of Dodo, is an example for us.[8] His mighty exploit was recorded to keep us from making the mistake that so many others have made. [9]

In this historical account, the army of King David had defied the Philistines to engage them in battle. The fact that this band of reformed outlaws (those who were in distress, in debt, and discontented[10]) defied the Philistines indicates they were probably greatly outnumbered. The odds were against them, but they presented themselves for battle. They conquered the first lie. It must have been an awesome moment.

What did the army of the king do after they rose up and presented themselves in the face of the impossible? The Scripture is clear—they retreated.[11] In modern terminology—they just quit! Obviously they took their eyes off of their king and looked at the multitude of men that were against them.

Nevertheless, Eleazar the son of Dodo (what a name) the Ahohite, did not quit. What did he do when all others retreated? Once again the Scripture is clear and precise, *"He arose and attacked the Philistines until his hand was weary, and his hand stuck to the sword."*[12]

Here was a man who was a nobody from nowhere. I've never heard of the land of Ahoh before or after him, have you? The man was not even an Israelite. He was an outlaw that had gathered himself to a royal king when the king was hiding in the cave of Adullam.[13]

Obviously his life had been transformed through his relationship with the royal King David—a man after God's own heart.[14] It is inherent in the power of royalty to bring out the best from the worst (Adino, the Eznite), and the strongest from the weakest (Eleazar, the Ahohite).

When all others had retreated, Eleazar arose and attacked the enemy. We could say that he attacked and conquered the second lie. He did not quit. In truth, the Word of God is precise saying, *"his hand stuck to the sword."*[15] Beyond human strength, beyond human ability, Eleazar became the strongest of all by sticking to what he had begun.

We should never simply read the Holy Scriptures as only an historical account of the past. The Word of God is the testimony of our great royal King, Jesus Christ.[16] Jesus said, *"'The words* [testimony] *that I speak to you are spirit, and they are life.'"*[17]

Considering the spirituality of God's Word, what application can we make of Eleazar's example? In the New Testament the sword of the Spirit is the Word of God.[18] Eleazar's hand stuck to the sword. We could say that Eleazar's hand stuck to the Word of God. Eleazar started with the Word, and stuck with the Word. This is the only way to conquer the second lie.

No matter what anyone else around you is doing, stick to God's Word. Don't quit! Keep your hand on the sword. *After you have done the will of God, you have need of endurance if you are to obtain the promised blessing.*[19] Don't quit! The apostle Peter declared,

> *Beloved, do not think it strange concerning the fiery trial* [the second lie] *which is to try you, as though some strange thing happened to you.*[20]

Remember, these are the words of Peter, the man who once got out of the boat and walked on water.[21] He too conquered the first lie. Remember the biblical account. After a while he began to sink as he took his eyes off the Lord and focused on the circumstances of wind and wave.[22] The second lie might have drowned him had he not stuck to the word of Jesus who had said, *"'Come.'"*[23] In conquering the second lie, Peter was able to put his hand into the hand of the Lord (the Word) and walk back to the boat safely with Him.[24]

The writer of the book of Hebrews encouraged the people of God saying,

> *Beloved, we are confident of better things* [than falling away—quitting] *concerning you, yes things that accompany salvation* [the conquering of the first lie], *though we speak in this manner* [don't quit]. *For God is not unjust to forget your work and labor of love which you have shown toward His name* [our royal King], *in that you have ministered to the saints, and do minister. And we desire that each one of you show the same diligence to the full assurance of hope until the end, that you do not become sluggish* [quit], *but imitate those* [Eleazar, Peter, and so many others] *who through faith and patience inherit the promises.*[25]

Do not quit; stick to the Word of God. You can conquer the first lie by acting on the Word, against all odds. You can conquer the second lie by *continuing* to act on the Word. Through his association with the royal king, Eleazar became great. The Lord is able to bring out the best from the worst, and the strongest from the weakest.

The royal edict commands, *"Watch, stand fast in the faith, be brave, be strong."*[26] We are commanded not to just start a good work, but to prove the promises of God by finishing it. We are commanded to *"hold fast"* until Jesus returns.[27]

By "holding fast" to the Word of God and not quitting, the blessings of God preserve our lives. The wisdom of the Proverbs is clear, *"Take fast hold of instruction* [the Word of God], *let her not go; keep her, for she is thy life."*[28]

The admonitions in the New Testament for holding fast and not quitting are numerous. Paul wrote, *"Prove all things; hold fast that which is good."*[29] He declared that we would be comforted by the Lord and established in every good word and work if we will stand fast and hold the traditions revealed in the Word of God.[30]

With complete confidence in our royal King, Jesus, Paul wrote to his son in the faith Timothy saying,

> *For I know whom I have believed and am persuaded that He is able to keep what I have committed to Him until that Day.*[31]

He went on to encourage Timothy to *hold fast* this pattern of sound words.[32]

The writer of the book of Hebrews encouraged believers to *"hold fast the confidence and the rejoicing of the hope firm to the end."*[33] We are to stick to the sword, *holding fast* the confession of our faith without wavering; for the great royal King who promised us the blessing is faithful and true.[34]

We can assuredly conquer the second lie of the devil by sticking to God's Word. The Word of God is alive and powerful, sharper than any two edged sword.[35] He who has the sharp two edged sword (Jesus our Lord) has this to say to us in the face of the lies of the devil, *"'I know your works, and where you dwell, where Satan's throne is. And you hold fast to My name . . ."*[36]

Remember how you started to do a good work. You acted in good faith on the Word of God that commanded, *"And whatever you do in word or deed, do all in the name of the Lord Jesus, giving thanks to God the Father through Him."*[37]

Don't quit now. Hold fast. Stick to it. By holding fast to the name of the Lord and continuing to do His Word without quitting, you become an overcomer. There is a promise for you, and for all who follow your example:

> *"To him who overcomes I will give some of the hidden manna to eat. And I will give him a white stone, and*

on the stone a new name written which no one knows except him who receives it."[38]

Eleazar went from being the son of Dodo to becoming one of King David's mighty men. Eleazar is a Hebrew name which means, "God is my helper."[39] It is written concerning him:

He arose and attacked the Philistines until his hand was weary, and his hand stuck to the sword. The Lord brought about a great victory that day; and the people returned after him only to plunder.[40]

Out of the weak came the strong. It is the nature of royalty to conquer satanic lies. Don't quit. It is very important for you, your family, and all who are observing your life. God can give you a new name—"more than a conqueror!"[41] You *can* finish what you start.

And let us not grow weary while doing good, for in due season we shall reap if we do not lose heart.
Galatians 6:9

CHAPTER 4: CONQUER THE SECOND LIE

Main Points:

- Endurance is necessary for a person to experience the fullness of God's blessing.
- Many people start a good work, but few finish it.
- After the devil's first lie, there is a second one—"Just quit!"
- Once you have started a good work, stick to it.
- God can bring forth the strongest from the weakest.
- Do not think it strange that you experience fiery trials.
- We inherit the promises through faith and patience.
- You can finish what you start.
- In due season, you will reap if you do not quit.

CHAPTER 5
CONQUER THE THIRD LIE

"The kingdom of heaven is like a treasure hidden in a field, which a man found and hid; and for joy over it he goes and sells all that he has and buys that field."
Matthew 13:44

And after him was Shammah the son of Agee the Hararite. The Philistines had gathered together into a troop where there was a piece of ground full of lentils. So the people fled from the Philistines.
2 Samuel 23:11

Here we go again. We conquered the first lie that told us, "You just can't do it." We conquered the second lie that told us, "Just quit." Then we hear lie number three, "It's just not worth it." Haven't you heard that before?

After you step out in faith and do the will of God and conquer the temptation to quit, you can be sure that the devil will try again to defeat you. His tactics are the same every time. We are not to be ignorant of his devices.[1]

Our help will once again come from the historical account of King David's mighty men. The royal character of the king can bring the best out of the worst, the strongest out of the weakest, and the most out of the least. Remember, whatever you do—do it in the name of the Lord with your whole heart, unto Him and not unto men.[2]

Shammah was the third mighty man of David. He was there when the Philistines assembled their warriors in a field of lentils.[3] Do you know what lentils are? They are beans. Lentils are a type of bean.[4] The battle was over a hill of beans!

Haven't you ever heard the saying, "That doesn't amount to a hill of beans"? What that means is, "It's just not worth it." That is a lie of the devil. The reason we fall for it is so obvious when reading the story of Shammah.

As we read, we can't help but ask the question, "What is the value of a piece of ground full of lentils?" What was Shammah thinking? Perhaps he was learning the way of royalty that can bring out the most from the least. The Scripture records the account saying, *"But he stationed himself in the middle of the field, defended it, and killed the Philistines."*[5]

If the story read that he stationed himself in a field full of diamonds or gold, it would make more sense to the natural mind; but a field full of beans? Obviously it's not worth risking one's life for. That's a lie.

The field that you and I are laboring in is nothing less than the whole world! This is exactly what Jesus taught in the great parable of the wheat and the tares. The disciples came to Him saying, *"'Explain to us the parable of the tares of the field.'"*[6] Jesus answered and said to them, *"'He who sows the good seed is the Son of Man. The field is the world ...'"*[7] This parable is all about the harvest[8] of what the Bible calls the *"precious fruit of the earth."*[9]

The field that Shammah stationed himself in probably didn't look like much. The piece of ground that sums up the whole of your own life may not look like much either when compared to the multitudes of people that come and go through it, treating it as such a worthless thing.

Take heart. What you are doing is changing the world. God has no other plan. We sometimes get so caught up with our faith in Him, that we forget the faith He has in us. He knows how to get the most out of the least of us.

God has done such a perfect work in and through Christ,[10] that He called Him back to heaven and left the whole field, full of earth people, in our hands.[11]

He knows that in the light of truth, we will see the value of this field. It is not full of beans—it is full of people.

This is the way of the kingdom of God. He hides a treasure in the midst of what looks like a worthless field.[12] When the Eternal Word was born some two thousand years ago, He came into this world in an obscure manner, and was laid in a little feeding trough for beasts. There was no room for Him to be born at the inn.[13] Who knew the real value of the miracle that was taking place in such an obscure place?

The Eternal Word became the Incarnate Word in nowheresville; nobodyville, if you understand what I mean. The royal anointing on Him was destined to make the most out of the least. What happened in that little corner of "beanville" changed the world forever.

When Jesus walked the earth, there were no televisions, no Internet websites, no e-mails, and no newspapers to report the great miracles He performed for people who didn't seem to be worth very much. He did it all in what could be called obscurity—a field of lentils.

Jesus was so much like everyone else. He was a common man. It was hard (for even the closest to Him) to recognize the value of His life, and what He was accomplishing for the multitudes of others who would believe in Him through the ages. They stumbled at His humble heritage saying, *"Is this not the carpenter's son?"*[14]

It was as if to mockingly ask, "What great value could the son of a common laborer possibly have?" Obviously Jesus didn't look like much more than a common lentil among a hill of beans. He had no form or comeliness, no beauty that would make anyone desire or esteem His value.[15] Yet He was certainly a treasure hidden in the field of the world.

So it was also with the death and burial of our Lord Jesus. The place where He was crucified and the place where He was buried, were nothing more than an obscure hill and a cave in the earth—a hill of beans. Yet what He did there and then changed the world forever.

The historical account of David's mighty man, Shammah, is a foreshadowing of the true value of the harvest field of the world that Christ died and rose again for. Shammah stationed himself in the middle of that field, defended it, and so to speak, conquered the third lie of Satan.[16] Shammah proved the value of that hill of beans. Through his great exploit the LORD brought about a great victory,[17] bringing forth the most from the least.

Let me tell it straight. Shammah stationed himself in the middle of the field. What are we waiting for? Let's station ourselves right in the middle of what God is doing in the earth.

It is essential for all Christians to come to the revelation that the field is the world and the lentils represent the harvest of precious souls. We, each one of us, must move to the center of what God is doing. Staying on the fringes, the borders of the field is not the place for a mighty one of God.

In the Old Testament agricultural economy, the LORD gave clear instruction concerning the harvest field. He instructed the laborers to reap the field in a particular way. He told them not to reap the corners of the field.[18] Why not?

The corners of the field were the places where the poor, the stranger, the fatherless, and the widow could come to gather for eating what was unreaped, and to glean the droppings of the harvest.[19] The food found there is for others, not us!

This wonderful plan revealed two great truths. The first truth was that the LORD was revealing the high value that He placed on those who were not yet a part of His kingdom. The second truth was a reminder to His own people to remember the time they labored as slaves—people of little value—in the land of Egypt.[20] It is time for us to remember where we came from, and in so doing highly esteem the value of others still living in the bean field!

Though we were dead in trespass and sins,[21] the Lord put a high value on our lives and paid for us with His own precious blood.[22] The giving of His life for ours did not establish the value of our lives—it confirmed it. Think about it.

Be a mighty warrior for our great King, Jesus! Be like Shammah and get right in the middle of your hill of beans. The fact that the devil also wants it should seal the deal. Obviously there is a treasure hidden there.

These words have changed my life. They can change yours as well. Although you were once related to Adam racially, never forget you are now related to royalty—the generation of Jesus Christ.[23] In Him and through Him you can enjoy all the blessings of Abraham[24] to whom we are related through redemption.

In and through Christ you can also fulfill the purposes of God in our generation as David did in his.[25] It is David who personified our relationship to the royalty of our Lord Jesus Christ.

The greatness of our King can bring the best out of the worst, the strongest out of the weakest, and the most out of the least. Whatever you do in word or deed, do it all in the name of Jesus, giving thanks to God the Father through Him.[26] You can do it. Don't quit. *"Whatever you do, do it heartily, as to the Lord and not to men."*[27] It is definitely worth it. Do it now.

> *"Do not say, 'There are still four months to harvest.' Behold I say to you, lift up your eyes and look at the fields, for they are already white for harvest!"*
> John 4:35 (paraphrased)

CHAPTER 5: CONQUER THE THIRD LIE

Main Points:

- After using his first two lies, the devil attacks with another lie—"It's just not worth it!"
- We are not ignorant of Satan's devices.
- God can bring out the most from the least.
- What you are doing may not look like much, but it is like a treasure hidden in a field.
- The field is the world.
- Station yourself in the middle of the field.
- Remember where you came from and the value of your own life.
- Esteem the lives of others in light of God's royal love.
- The field is already ripe for harvest.

EPILOGUE

TURN WATER TO WINE

On the third day there was a wedding in Cana of Galilee . . . . when they ran out of wine . . . . His mother said, "Whatever He says to you, do it." Jesus said to them, "Fill the waterpots with water . . . . Draw some out . . . take it to the master of the feast." The water was made wine. This beginning of signs Jesus did in Cana of Galilee, and manifested His glory; and His disciples believed in Him.
John 2:1-11 (excerpts)

And David said with longing, "Oh, that someone would give me a drink of the water from the well of Bethlehem [the house of bread[1]] which is by the gate!"
2 Samuel 23:15

Hunger and thirst are experienced by everyone. This is because eating and drinking are as essential to life as breathing—only not as immediate. Think about it. If you stop breathing you will die quickly. If you stop eating and drinking it will take longer, but you will soon be just as dead.

Hunger and thirst are common to man. It is not just natural nourishment that mankind needs and desires. There is a spiritual food and drink that all human beings require and search for.

Our heavenly Father, the Creator of everything, prescribed both a natural and spiritual diet for man. Just as it is important in the natural to eat and drink properly, so it is in the spiritual realm.

The LORD God prescribed spiritual bread for man saying, *"'Man shall not live by bread alone; but by every word that proceeds from the mouth of the LORD.'"*[2] Jesus also taught that there is spiritual water that God has prescribed for man to drink. To the woman at the well of Samaria Jesus said,

> *"But whoever drinks of the water that I shall give him will never thirst. But the water that I shall give him will become in him a fountain of water springing up into everlasting life."*[3]

Without fulfilling the spiritual need and desire to eat and drink, the souls of men faint within them. They wander in the wilderness (of this world) in a desolate way, crying out in distress.[4] They have need of a Savior and loving King.

> *Oh, that men would give thanks to the LORD for His goodness, And for His wonderful works to the children of men! For He satisfies the longing soul, And fills the hungry soul with goodness.*[5]

Even our Lord Jesus Christ experienced this spiritual hunger and thirst. After being tempted in the wilderness for forty days by the devil, the Scripture says that He was hungry.[6] His temptation probably included conquering some form of the three lies of Satan that I have written about. He was tempted in all points as we are, yet without sin.[7]

The response of Jesus to the devil concerning breaking His fast by turning a stone to bread, showed that He hungered not just for natural food, but to see the will of God done. He quoted the Old Testament written Word saying, *"'Man shall not live by bread alone, but by every word of God.'"*[8]

It is the same concerning thirst. The thirst that Jesus experienced during His encounter with the woman at the well of Samaria was for far more than a natural drink. He began His discourse with the woman saying, *"'Give Me a drink.'"*[9]

The outcome of this encounter makes the context of His statement clear. Jesus was really talking about *"living water"*[10] and His thirst to satisfy the Father's desire for the great harvest of souls. He said, *"'My food* [and drink] *is to do the will of Him who sent Me, and to finish His work.'"*[11]

Then Jesus immediately drew the attention of His disciples to the harvest fields that were already white and ready to be reaped.[12] The woman at the well had left her waterpot, gone into the city,[13] and brought a multitude of hungry and thirsty people to meet Him.[14] Many of the Samaritans (bean field people) believed in Him and were harvested into the kingdom of God.[15]

At the conclusion of His life—at the moment of His death Jesus cried out, *"'I thirst!'"*[16] He was crying out once again to see the will of God completely fulfilled concerning the salvation of mankind. With His last breath, when He had received the sour wine (the Gethsemane cup of exceeding sorrow, even to death; the will of the Father [17]) He said, *"'It is finished!'"*[18] and bowing His head he gave up His spirit.[19] This was His final act in releasing the water of life to whoever thirsts.[20]

It is written, *"'Blessed are those who hunger and thirst for righteousness, For they shall be filled.'"*[21] We could say that their hunger and thirst is to fulfill the will of God. This is the hunger and thirst that is essential to all spiritual life.

Those who provide food for the hungry and drink for the thirsty thus fulfilling God's Word, are blessed by the Father and inherit the kingdom of God.[22] Jesus prepared the way for us and commands us to follow Him into the harvest field of the world.[23] When we provide this spiritual food and drink to the least of those that Jesus came and died for, we do it to Him.[24] How great a salvation![25]

The historical account of King David and his mighty men foreshadowed our relationship with the Lord Jesus Christ, and our relationship to Him as laborers in the harvest field of the world. It is recorded that at the time of harvest three of King David's mighty men came to him at the cave of Adullam while a troop of Philistines had encamped in the valley.[26]

The details of this encounter are extremely important. The Philistines had their garrison (the strength of their army) in the city of Bethlehem (the house of bread).[27] David said with longing,

"Oh, that someone would give me a drink of the water from the well of Bethlehem, which is by the gate!"[28]

This cry from the heart of David was very similar to what the Lord Jesus said when at the Samaritan well. He said, *"'Give Me a drink.'"*[29] and from the cross He cried out, *"'I thirst!'"*[30] Is anyone listening to such a spiritual cry? Is *anyone* ready to become *someone*? Are *you* ready?

The scriptural account tells us that three of David's mighty men (perhaps those that conquered the three lies) heard him cry out and at the risk of their own lives, broke through the entire encampment of the Philistines. They drew water from the well of Bethlehem that was by the gate and brought it back to King David.[31]

Nevertheless, David would not drink it, but poured it out to the LORD.[32] David said,

"Far be it from me, O LORD, that I should do this! Is this [water] not the blood of the men who went [into the harvest field] in jeopardy of their lives?"[33]

David understood what an impossible task these three mighty men had set out to do. He understood that not only had they broken through the enemy's stronghold, but they had not stopped at that. There was no quit in them. They had kept going. They had drawn water from the well and returned it to their king. David knew that these three mighty men had come to understand the value of their king's desire for the waters of life from the well at the house of bread.

Just as it is written that man shall not live by bread alone,[34] it is also written,

'For the life of the flesh is in the blood, and I have given it to you upon the altar to make atonement for your soul; for it is the blood that makes atonement for the soul.'[35]

It is time for us to recognize the New Testament significance of the water from the well at the house of bread.

The bread of Christ's broken body (from Bethlehem, the house of bread) along with the wine (His blood) has become our covenant meal.[36] Without eating and drinking this covenant meal, we have no life in us.[37] Now that we eat and drink and are filled with His righteousness, we live and move and have our being in Him.[38] Therefore, in His name, with our whole hearts, let us continually provide food and drink for the least of those among us.[39] In so doing we will fulfill and fill full the good pleasure of His will.

Finally, in the Old Testament, David recognized that the water from Bethlehem's well was like the lifeblood of his three mighty men. In the New Testament, Jesus recognized that the water at the wedding of Cana of Galilee was an opportunity to cause men to believe in Him. He manifested His glory through a wonderful beginning of signs as He turned the water into wine which signified His life blood.[40]

Since we are Christ's disciples and our own lives are for signs and wonders,[41] let us do the same as David's mighty men did. We too can overcome the lies of the devil. As we do it's like bringing our Lord Jesus what He's longing for – a drink of water from the well at the house of bread. To use a well-worn saying from our natural culture, He will do much more than make lemonade out of a lemon, He will change the water into wine!

And so in closing, I'm going to act now on what He's saying to me. In the name of the Lord Jesus Christ, with my whole heart, I call you great and mighty in the name of He who is Great and Mighty. I call *you* the children of the Most High God. I call *you* His princes and princesses in all the earth. I call *you* laborers in the harvest field of the world. I call you *more than conquerors* through Him who loves us.[42]

I tell you, concerning the Christ life in you, "Yes, you can. Don't quit. It's worth it!" It's just like at the wedding of Cana. The secret has been revealed. Somewhere between our obedience and the presentation of the water to the master of the feast (Lord of the harvest[43]) a miracle takes place! The water turns to wine. Live for an audience of One!

"Whatever He says to you, do it."
John 2:5b

EPILOGUE: TURN WATER TO WINE

Main Points:

- Hunger and thirst are experienced by everyone.
- Eating and drinking are as essential to life as breathing—only not as immediate.
- The concept of eating and drinking can be spiritually understood.
- Even Jesus Christ experienced hunger and thirst.
- Man can only satisfy his spiritual hunger and thirst by fulfilling God's will.
- As we bring food and water to the hungry and thirsty, we bring it to Jesus.
- It costs us our lives to bring food and water to the hungry and thirsty.
- We honor our King when we spend our lives to fulfill His will.
- This honor is a true sign and wonder that will cause others to believe in Christ.
- You are great and mighty in Christ.
- Live for an audience of One!

WORKS CITED

Prologue: GO AND SIN NO MORE

1. John 3:3
2. Ephesians 2:1
3. John 3:7
4. John 1:13
5. Romans 5:23
6. Romans 8:2
7. Romans 8:1
8. John 8:3-4
9. John 8:5-6
10. John 8:7-9
11. John 8:11b
12. John 1:13
13. Mark 16:15
14. Matthew 28:19
15. Matthew 10:8b
16. John 8:31, 32
17. John 8:36
18. Galatians 5:1
19. Matthew 9:37-38; Matthew 13:38a
20. Isaiah 8:18; Hebrews 2:13b; Mark 16:17-18
21. Revelation 12:10
22. John 8:44

23. 2 Peter 1:2
24. 2 Corinthians 2:11
25. Romans 1:16
26. 1 Corinthians 12:27 KJV
27. 2 Corinthians 5:8; 1 Thessalonians 4:17
28. John 1:13
29. Acts 1:8
30. Romans 8:37
31. Ephesians 1:19-21
32. John 2:9-11
33. John 2:5
34. James 1:25
35. James 1:22
36. James 2:17, 26
37. Acts 1:3
38. Revelation 21:5
39. Ephesians 5:14
40. Luke 4:3, 9 paraphrased
41. Philippians 4:13
42. 2 Corinthians 10:5
43. Ephesians 6:16
44. Ephesians 6:11, 13
45. 1 Corinthians 16:13
46. James 4:7
47. 1 Peter 5:9a
48. Galatians 5:1
49. John 8:11

Chapter 1: WHATEVER YOU DO

1. Hebrews 10:7
2. Psalm 35:27
3. Ibid
4. John 8:28-29
5. Matthew 3:17; 17:5

6. John 5:19
7. John 5:20; Mark 14:36; 2 Peter 3:9; John 3:16
8. John 15:4, 8
9. John 15:5
10. John 14:12
11. Luke 12:32; 1 Corinthians 12:12; Luke 11:2
12. 1 Corinthians 12:27 KJV
13. Genesis 1:27; Romans 8:29
14. John 15:16
15. Psalm 1:1-3
16. John 13:17
17. James 1:25
18. Philippians 4:13
19. Colossians 3:17
20. Luke 9:1-2; Mark 16:15-20
21. Philippians 2:9-11
22. Acts 4:12
23. 1 Peter 1:9
24. Hebrews 12:2
25. Romans 10:17
26. Joshua 1:8-9
27. Ecclesiastes 4:12
28. John 3:16
29. Colossians 3:17
30. Psalm 11:4; 95:2
31. Psalm 16:11
32. Colossians 3:17
33. Psalm 92:1
34. 2 Corinthians 2:14
35. Proverbs 16:7
36. Hebrews 11:6
37. Psalm 41:11
38. Colossians 3:23
39. Source unknown
40. Matthew 26:39

41. Revelation 3:16
42. John 15:8
43. Psalm 18:3
44. Psalm 9:1
45. Psalm 111:1-2; NKJV and KJV
46. Matthew 22:36
47. Matthew 22:37
48. Matthew 22:39
49. Deuteronomy 6:4-5 KJV
50. Deuteronomy 6:7
51. Deuteronomy 6:8
52. Malachi 1:6
53. Malachi 1:7-8a paraphrased excerpts
54. Malachi 1:8b
55. Numbers 32:23
56. Proverbs 4:23
57. Colossians 3:17, 23; James 1:25 paraphrased excerpts
58. Romans 8:14
59. John 13:35
60. Matthew 22:36-39
61. James 2:8
62. John 15:16
63. 1 Peter 2:9a

Chapter 2: DISCOVER THE ROYAL RELATIONSHIP

1. John 14:6
2. John 1:14
3. Revelation 17:14
4. Matthew 3:17
5. Romans 8:29
6. Hebrews 2:19
7. John 17:17
8. Hebrews 2:11

9. Hebrews 2:13b
10. Isaiah 8:18a
11. Mark 16:17
12. Revelation 1:11a; Hebrews 1:1-3
13. Hebrews 12:2
14. Matthew 16:13
15. Galatians 3:16
16. Matthew 1:1 KJV
17. John 7:42; Romans 1:3
18. Colossians 3:23
19. Acts 2:36
20. 1 Corinthians 10:11
21. Genesis 2:7
22. Luke 2:6-7
23. Matthew 16:13
24. Romans 3:23
25. Romans 5:12
26. Genesis 5:3
27. John 1:1, 14
28. Isaiah 7:14
29. Hebrews 1:5
30. 1 Corinthians 15:45, 47
31. Colossians 1:18
32. Matthew 1:1 KJV
33. Acts 17:26a
34. Revelations 5:9
35. 2 Corinthians 5:17
36. Romans 4:11
37. Galatians 3:16
38. Genesis 11:31; 15:7
39. Genesis 17:1
40. Romans 4:22
41. Genesis 12:3; Galatians 3:8
42. Genesis 15:8-10, 17
43. Galatians 3:16

44. Revelation 5:9
45. John 3:16
46. 1 Samuel 13:14
47. Matthew 1:1; 9:27
48. John 7:42; Romans 1:3; 2 Timothy 2:8
49. Colossians 3:23 paraphrased
50. Revelation 5:9-10
51. 1 Peter 2:9a
52. 1 Corinthians 1:26
53. 1 Corinthians 1:27-28
54. 1 Samuel 22:2
55. 1 Samuel 15:28
56. Romans 8:37

Chapter 3: CONQUER THE FIRST LIE

1. 1 Samuel 22:2
2. 1 Corinthians 10:11
3. Romans 15:4
4. Genesis 1:1; 2:7; John 1:4; 14:6
5. A Child is Born; Lennart Nilsson, Lars Hamberger; copyright 2003, Page 52
6. Ibid, Page 30
7. Ibid, Page 65
8. Ibid, Page 25
9. Jeremiah 1:4-5a
10. Acts 10:34; Romans 2:11; Ephesians 6:9; Colossians 3:25 all in KJV
11. Ibid
12. James 2:9
13. James 2:8
14. Hebrews 11:6
15. Jeremiah 1:5a; Psalm 139:13, 15-16
16. Jeremiah 1:5b
17. Psalm 139:14-16

18. Philippians 4:13
19. Psalm 139:17
20. Psalm 139:18

Chapter 4: CONQUER THE SECOND LIE

1. 1 Peter 2:11
2. 1 Peter 2:12
3. Matthew 14:29
4. 2 Peter 1:1
5. 1 Peter 3:1
6. Ibid
7. Hebrews 10:36
8. 2 Samuel 23:9a
9. 1 Corinthians 10:6
10. 1 Samuel 22:2
11. 2 Samuel 23:9b
12. 2 Samuel 23:10a
13. 1 Samuel 22:1
14. 1 Samuel 13:14
15. 2 Samuel 23:10a
16. John 5:39
17. John 6:63
18. Ephesians 6:17
19. Hebrews 10:36
20. 1 Peter 4:12
21. Matthew 14:29
22. Matthew 14:30
23. Matthew 14:29a
24. Matthew 14:31-32
25. Hebrews 6:9-12
26. 1 Corinthians 16:13
27. Revelation 2:25
28. Proverbs 4:13 KJV
29. 1 Thessalonians 5:21 KJV

30. 2 Thessalonians 2:15-17
31. 2 Timothy 1:12b
32. 2 Timothy 1:13
33. Hebrews 3:6b
34. Hebrew 10:23 KJV; Revelation 19:11
35. Hebrews 4:12a
36. Revelation 2:12-13a
37. Colossians 3:17
38. Revelation 2:17b
39. Strong's Exhaustive Concordance of the Bible; Hebrew Dictionary, word #499
40. 2 Samuel 23:10
41. Romans 8:37

Chapter 5: CONQUER THE THIRD LIE

1. 2 Corinthians 2:11
2. Colossians 3:17, 23
3. 2 Samuel 23:1
4. "lentil." (2008) In Merriam-Webster Online Dictionary. Retrieved November 8, 2008, from http://www.merriam-webster.com/dictionary/lentil
5. 2 Samuel 23:12a
6. Matthew 13:36
7. Matthew 13: 37-38a
8. Matthew 13:39
9. James 5:7
10. John 19:30
11. Acts 1:9-11; Matthew 28:18-20; Mark 16:15
12. Matthew 13:44
13. Luke 2:7
14. Matthew 13:55
15. Isaiah 53:2
16. 2 Samuel 23:12b
17. 2 Samuel 23:12b

18. Leviticus 19:9
19. Leviticus 19:10; Deuteronomy 24:19-21
20. Deuteronomy 24:22
21. Ephesians 2:1
22. 1 Peter 1:18-19
23. 2 Corinthians 5:17
24. Galatians 3:14
25. Acts 13:36
26. Colossians 3:17
27. Colossians 3:23

Epilogue: TURN WATER TO WINE

1. Strong's Exhaustive Concordance of the Bible; Hebrew Dictionary, word #1035
2. Deuteronomy 8:3b; Luke 4:4
3. John 4:14
4. Psalm 107:4-6
5. Psalm 107:8-9
6. Luke 4:2
7. Hebrews 4:15
8. Luke 4:4
9. John 4:7
10. John 4:10
11. John 4:34
12. John 4:35
13. John 4:28
14. John 4:30
15. John 4:39
16. John 19:28
17. Matthew 26:38-39
18. John 19:30
19. John 19:30
20. Revelation 21:6
21. Matthew 5:6

22. Matthew 25:34b
23. Matthew 4:19
24. Matthew 25:40
25. Hebrews 2:3
26. 2 Samuel 23:13
27. 2 Samuel 23:14
28. 2 Samuel 23:15
29. John 4:7
30. John 19:28
31. 2 Samuel 23:16
32. Ibid
33. 2 Samuel 23:17
34. Luke 4:4
35. Leviticus 17:11
36. 1 Corinthians 11:23-26
37. John 6:53
38. Acts 17:28a
39. Matthew 25:40
40. John 2:11, 9a
41. Isaiah 8:18
42. Romans 8:37
43. Matthew 9:38

www.ingramcontent.com/pod-product-compliance
Ingram Content Group UK Ltd.
Pitfield, Milton Keynes, MK11 3LW, UK
UKHW041948230426
12048UKWH00008B/211